Lerner SPORTS

EXTREME SPEED

SUPERFAST MOTORCYCLE RACING

Janet Slingerland

Lerner Publications Company
An imprint of Lerner Publishing Group, Inc.
241 First Avenue North
Minneapolis, MN 55401 USA

For reading levels and more information, look up this title at www.lernerbooks.com.

Main body text set in Myriad Pro.
Typeface provided by Adobe.

Library of Congress Cataloging-in-Publication Data

Names: Slingerland, Janet, author.
Title: Superfast motorcycle racing / Janet Slingerland.
Description: Minneapolis : Lerner Publications, 2020. | Series: Extreme speed (Learner sports) | Includes bibliographical references and index. | Audience: Ages 7–11 (provided by Lerner Publications) | Audience: Grades 2–3 (provided by Lerner Publications)
Identifiers: LCCN 2019026115 (print) | LCCN 2019026114 (ebook) | ISBN 9781541577213 (library binding) | ISBN 9781541587380 (paperback) | ISBN 9781541582934 (ebook)
Subjects: LCSH: Motorcycle racing—Juvenile literature.
Classification: LCC GV1060 .S567 2020 (ebook) | LCC GV1060.12 .S58 2019 (print) | DDC 796.7/5—dc23

LC record available at https://lccn.loc.gov/2019026115

CONTENTS

CHAPTER 1

THE GRAND PRIX

MotoGP racers speed around turns while their bodies hover mere inches off the track.

Riders lined up their motorcycles on the starting grid at Motorland Aragon in Alcañiz, Spain, in September 2018. They revved their engines. The crowd of 63,000 people cheered. The green flag waved, and the motorcycles took off. The Aragon **Grand Prix** was under way.

FACTS AT A GLANCE

- Some motorcycles cost between $2 million and $3.5 million each.

- Riders lose about a half gallon (2 L) of sweat in each race.

- MotoGP riders have airbags in their suits. The airbags take only 45 milliseconds (0.045 seconds) to inflate.

- During race weekend, the fastest 10 racers in the practice race skip directly to the second qualifying race, called Q2. The slower riders compete in the first qualifying race, called Q1.

MotoGP drivers carefully balance their bikes as they navigate the corners of the track.

The racers battled for position on the track. At the first turn, one rider crashed. The rest raced on. Italian Andrea Dovizioso took the lead while reigning world champion Marc Márquez and Andrea Iannone traded places behind Dovizioso.

The riders leaned into each corner. Their knees and elbows hovered just above the track. Dovizioso and Márquez moved back and forth between first and second place positions.

At one turn, Iannone raced past the others, but Dovizioso quickly took the lead again. Márquez fell back to third. On the straightaway, Márquez opened the **throttle**. He snuck past Iannone to race against Dovizioso. In the end, Márquez rode to victory. Dovizioso finished less than a second later and Iannone followed right behind.

Márquez celebrated his win at the Aragon Grand Prix with a victory lap while waving his flag.

MotoGP riders have to watch out for the other riders on the track and make sure that they do not crash.

This is the world of MotoGP racing. These events are dangerous and unpredictable. Top racers compete at breakneck speeds. They soar around the track. During turns, drivers almost touch the ground because they lean over so far. Fans gasp in shock and awe when the motorcycles zoom past the stands.

Motorcyclists started racing in the early 1900s. In 1949, the International Motorcycle Federation crowned the first world champion. Since then, the federation has governed the top motorcycle racing events in the world. The first 15 riders in these races earn points toward the world championship. The MotoGP championship consists of 19 races that take place in 15 countries around the world.

Early racing motorcycles looked very different from the MotoGP bikes seen today.

In the beginning, there were multiple single-rider classes. Riders could race in more than one class at a time. This helped Giacomo Agostini win the most titles in history. He won 15 total titles, 10 of which he won between 1968 and 1972.

MotoGP riders can perform wheelies on their motorcycles. This is when the front tire pops off the track and the motorcycle moves forward only on the rear tire.

Today, MotoGP has four levels, but riders typically only participate in one level at a time. MotoGP is the highest level of racing. The bikes are the fastest. Moto2 and Moto3 lead up to MotoGP. These bikes are slower. MotoE is a separate class for electric motorcycles. But fans of all ages love the four MotoGP classes for one reason: the thrill of the race makes MotoGP one of the most exciting motorsports in the world!

Crashes are common in motorcycle races. During the 2018 season, there were 1,077 crashes among the MotoGP levels.

CHAPTER 2

THE RACING MOTORCYCLE

MotoGP motorcycles are not available to the average consumer. They are custom built with the latest technology.

People hold umbrellas over MotoGP bikes on the starting grid. This keeps the fuel tank from overheating in the sun before the race.

MotoGP motorcycles are built so they can speed around the twists and turns of grand prix race tracks. They need to be light and durable. The materials used include titanium and carbon fiber, which are usually very expensive. The bikes are high tech too. They have 30 to 50 sensors that gather data such as fuel usage, engine power, throttle position, and lean angle. Large teams, sometimes called factory teams, have the best motorcycles. They can cost over $2 million each.

Fuel usage is one of the most important parts of MotoGP racing. Each bike has a 5.8-gallon (22 L) fuel tank. Tracks are different lengths, so racers must manage their fuel use to finish the race without running out.

MotoGP tires are slick. This texture helps the bikes reach top speeds around the track.

MotoGP provides the tires each racer uses. Each team gets a set number of tires for the entire race weekend. The front tires are usually hard, while the rear tires are softer. Soft tires provide more **grip** on the track.

MotoGP bikes have protective guards called fairings on the front to make them more **aerodynamic**. Fairings are connected to the body of the bike. They redirect large gusts of wind around the bike. They also protect the riders from dirt and debris. Fairings display the rider's team name, colors, and number.

Drivers use many buttons and switches on the handlebars to keep the bike operating correctly during the race.

Motorcycles in the MotoGP class have over 250 **horsepower**. The bike's powerful motor and lightweight body means that the average speed during a **premier** race is over 210 miles (338 km) per hour.

Crashing at that speed can do serious damage. Riders wear protective gear to help keep crashes from becoming deadly. They wear special boots, gloves, and helmets. They also have full-body **racing leathers** with extra padding in the shoulders, elbows, and knees. They fit like a second skin. The inner lining can be removed and washed. This is a must, since riders lose about 0.5 gallons (2 L) of sweat in each race.

REALLY?!

Some racing leathers are made from kangaroo hide. Others are made from cowhide. All leathers have extra padding. This padding in the shoulders, knees, and elbow protectors uses a special type of plastic that is hard on the inside and softer and rounder on the outside. The racing leathers weigh about 10 pounds (4.5 kg).

MotoGP riders also have airbags in their suits. Sensors determine if the airbags need to deploy. The airbags take just 45 milliseconds (0.045 seconds) to inflate. Special boots, gloves, and helmets complete the gear protecting the racers.

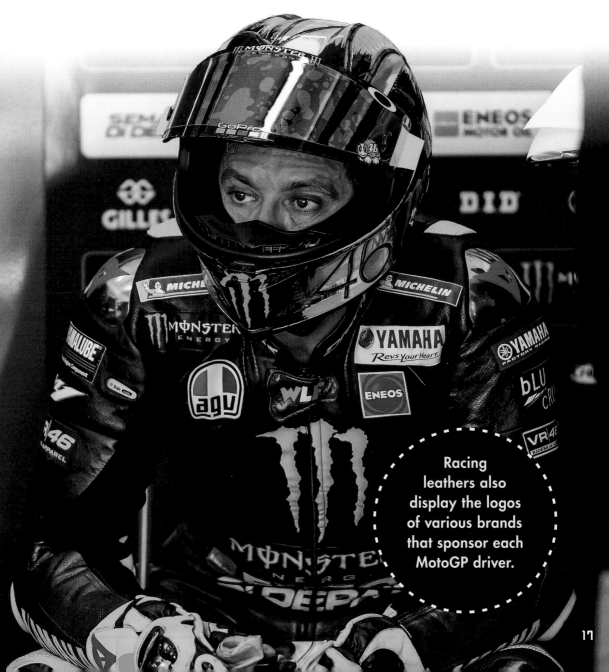

Racing leathers also display the logos of various brands that sponsor each MotoGP driver.

CHAPTER 3

PREPARING FOR THE RACE

Crews improve each MotoGP bike before the race.

The rider is the most visible part of a MotoGP team, but all members of the team are important leading up to the race. Off the track, engineers look for ways to modify the motorcycles to make them faster. Mechanics tune the motorcycles and make small changes that help the rider feel more comfortable during the race. Data engineers collect and analyze data to help mechanics and riders find the best motorcycle setup.

The pit box for a large team may have multiple motorcycles per driver.

During the off-season, riders train to keep their bodies fit. Many work with physical trainers. They run, ride bicycles and dirt bikes, and box. Riders work with the engineers and mechanics to make improvements to their motorcycles. Once the season starts, riders race about every two weeks.

A MotoGP race is really a three-day race weekend. One of the first things the team does is set up its **pit box**. There, the mechanics perform maintenance on the motorcycles. This includes tearing down and rebuilding bikes, cleaning and replacing parts, and checking sensors.

SPEED

VALENTINO ROSSI. In 2019, Valentino Rossi turned 40 years old. He also started his 24th year of world championship racing. Rossi has lived up to the promise he showed at a young age. He has won nine world championships.

In addition to competing, Rossi hosts riders at The Ranch, his Italian dirt-bike track. He also co-runs a riding academy, as well as Moto2 and Moto3 race teams.

Starting on Friday, the track is busy with practices and qualifying runs. Speeds in practice determine which qualifying race riders compete in. The fastest 10 racers in practice skip directly to the second qualifying race, called Q2. The slower riders compete in the first qualifying race, called Q1.

Starting in pole position gives the rider a huge advantage over the other bikes at the beginning of the race.

The two fastest racers from the Q1 race then join the others for Q2. How racers place in the Q2 race determines their starting positions for the grand prix. All drivers want to earn the **pole position** to lead the pack on race day. Fridays and Saturdays are full of exciting races, but fans and racing teams look forward to Sunday, when the MotoGP final will take place.

Rider Sam Lowes (*right*) posed for photos with fans before a grand prix in Valencia, Spain.

Race weekends offer chances for fans to meet riders. Riders may sign autographs. Fans can test demo bikes. They can also watch riders in the Globe of Death. These riders race inside a giant steel ball. They travel upside down. It is dangerous to perform but exciting to watch.

Race weekends culminate in the grand prix race on Sunday. Teams prep the motorcycles to make sure the riders will be safe. Riders climb on and make their way to the starting grid. They rev the engines.

The crowd cheers as the riders do a warm-up lap around the track. Then they watch the red light above the starting line. When the light goes out, the race begins! The engines roar as the motorcycles take off. Many riders come to race, but at the end of the weekend, only one can be the winner.

Mugello Circuit features wide turns, including one final turn right before the finish line.

The Mugello Circuit in Tuscany, Italy, is home to one of the most energetic race weekends in MotoGP. More than 100,000 fans come to this track to cheer the racers on. Fans of Italian Valentino Rossi are well represented here. The grandstands are a sea of yellow, his racing color.

Some local races also occur during MotoGP race weekends. At the Circuit of the Americas in Texas, the MotoAmerica Superbike series competes during MotoGP weekend too. Fans can experience different levels of racing. They get excited hearing the loud engines.

REALLY?!

MotoGP racers lean so far into turns, their elbows may drag along the track. Lean angles in MotoGP reach about 64 degrees. At these extreme angles, the amount of tire in contact with the track is only around the size of a coin.

MotoGP is constantly changing. One major change has been the introduction of a new class of electric bikes, known as MotoE. These all-electric bikes first raced officially in July 2019. Industry professionals believe that electric motorcycles will offer new ways for MotoGP riders and fans to get excited about the sport. Regardless of MotoGP's future, one thing is certain: the bikes will remain out-of-this-world fast as they race down the track.

MotoE bikes are more environmentally friendly than standard MotoGP bikes.

MOTORCYCLE RACING
FAMILY TREE

Benelli 350/4, 1970s

MotoGP bikes have changed drastically over the years, but one thing has stayed the same—they're made to go fast!

Suzuki RGB500
Mark 8, 1980s

Yamaha YZR500, 2000s

Honda RC213V, 2010s

GLOSSARY

aerodynamic

travels better and faster due to the way it moves through air

grand prix

a racing event lasting over three days and involving multiple classes, consisting of two days of practicing and qualifying followed by a day of races

grip

the ability of a tire to adhere to the track

horsepower

a unit of measurement for the power of an engine

pit box

the team's home base during the MotoGP weekend where repairs are also made

pole position

the front-most starting position in the starting grid

premier

best or most important

racing leathers

full-body suits, usually leather, made to protect motorcycle racers' bodies during races

throttle

a valve that changes the amount of fuel going to the engine to change the speed of the motorcycle

FURTHER INFORMATION

Brooklyn, Billie. *Motorcycle Racing*. New York: PowerKids Press, 2015.

Ciovacco, Justine. *All About Motorcycles*. New York: Rosen, 2017.

Farndon, John. *Megafast Motorcycles*. Minneapolis: Hungry Tomato, 2016.

International Motorcycle Federation
http://www.fim-live.com/en

MotoGP
http://www.motogp.com

Wonderopolis: Why Don't Motorcycles Fall While Moving?
https://www.wonderopolis.org/wonder/why-dont-motorcycles-fall-while-moving

INDEX

PHOTO ACKNOWLEDGMENTS

The images in this book are used with the permission of: © mooinblack/Shutterstock.
com, pp. 4, 6; © Dan74/Shutterstock.com, pp. 5, 15, 29 (bottom right); © Mirco Lazzari
gp/Getty Images Sport/Getty Images, pp. 7, 8, 25; © Marka/Universal Images Group/
Getty Images, pp. 9, 29 (top left); © Nufa Qaiesz/Shutterstock.com, p. 10; © David
Ramos/Getty Images Sport/Getty Images, p. 11; © Mau47/Shutterstock.com, p. 12;
© daykung/Shutterstock.com, pp. 13, 22–23; © Robert Michael/AFP/Getty Images,
p. 14; © Hafiz Johari/Shutterstock.com, pp. 17, 19; © Natursports/Shutterstock.com,
p. 18; © Rainer Herhaus/Shutterstock.com, p. 20; © Graham Conaty Photography/
Shutterstock.com, p. 21; © Francesc Juan/Shutterstock.com, p. 24; © Claudio
Giovannini/Ansa/AP Images, p. 26; © Giandomenico Papello/Shutterstock.com, p. 28;
© Bob Thomas Sports Photography/Getty Images, p. 29 (top right); © Pascal Rondeau
/Allsport/Getty Images Sport/Getty Images, p. 29 (bottom left).

Front Cover: © Chris Covatta/Getty Images Sport/Getty Images.